GREAT EXPLORATIONS

Francisco Pizarro

The Conquest of Peru

Milton Meltzer

BENCHMARK BOOKS

MARSHALL CAVENDISH
NEW YORK

With special thanks to Professor Pablo Piccato, Columbia University, for his careful reading of this manuscript.

Benchmark Books
99 White Plains Road
Tarrytown, NY 10591-9001
www.marshallcavendish.com

Library of Congress Cataloging-in-Publication Data

Meltzer, Milton, 1915–
Francisco Pizarro : the conquest of Peru / by Milton Meltzer.
p. cm. — (Great explorations)
Summary: Introduces the life of the explorer who was sent to Peru in the sixteenth century by the king of Spain to conquer the Incas and claim their land and wealth for the Spanish crown.
Includes bibliographical references and index.
ISBN 0–7614–1607–2
1. Pizarro, Francisco, ca. 1475–1541—Juvenile literature. 2. Peru—History—Conquest, 1522–1548—Juvenile literature. 3. South America—Discovery and exploration—Spanish—Juvenile literature. 4. Incas—Juvenile literature. 5. Explorers—Peru—Biography—Juvenile literature. 6. Explorers—Spain—Biography—Juvenile literature. [1.Pizarro, Francisco, ca. 1475–1541. 2. Explorers. 3.Peru—History—Conquest, 1522–1548. 4. South America—Discovery and exploration—Spanish. 5. Incas. 6. Indians of South America.] I. Title .II. Series.

F3442.P776M45 2003
985'.02'092—dc21
2002156000

Photo Research by Candlepants Incorporated

Cover Photo: The Art Archive / Biblioteca Nacional Madrid / Dagli Orti
Cover Inset: North Wind Picture Archive
The photographs in this book are used by permission and through the courtesy of; *Bridgeman Art Library* : The Royal Geographical Society, London, U.K., 5. *North Wind Picture Archive* : 8, 26, 31, 37, 40, 47, 48, 53, 55, 61, 63. *Art Resource*, NY : Erich Lessing, 9; Michel Zabe, 16; Reunion des Musees Nationaux, 19; Tate Gallery, London, 28; Werner Forman, 42; Victoria and Albert Museum, London, 57. *Corbis* : 65; Bettmann, 13, 21, 24; Gianni Dagli Orti, 36; Historical Picture Archive, 38. *The Art Archive* : Alcazar Seville / Dagli Orti, 14; Biblioteca d'Ajuda Lisbon / Dagli Orti, 32; Archaeological Museum Lima / Dagli Orti, 33; Museuo Pedro de Osma Lima / Mireille Vautier, 36; Archaeological Museum Lima / Mireille Vautier, 39; Coll Abric de Vivero Lima / Mireille Vautier, 71; Museo 20 de Julio 1810 Bogota / Dagli Orti, 73.

Printed in China
1   3   5   6   4   2

Contents

foreword

Today when you look at a map of the world, you see seven continents, connected to one another by the seas. But if you were studying geography 500 years ago, the map of the world would look very different. It would show only three continents—Europe, Asia, and Africa.

What happened to the other four? North America? South America? Australia? Antarctica?

They existed and so did the millions of people who lived on those continents. However, sea routes from ocean to ocean around the world, connecting all the continents and their inhabitants, had not yet been fully discovered. Not until late in the fifteenth century would that begin to happen.

This is where Francisco Pizarro's story opens. He was one of the adventurers who sailed across oceans and found parts of the world

A map of the world, dated 1540

Europeans did not know existed. Some have called their "discovery" of the Western Hemisphere "the greatest event in history."

When Pizarro invaded the land we now call Peru, it was dominated by the Inca Empire. The empire stretched 2,500 miles (4,000 km) along the west coast of South America and was hundreds of miles wide.

foreword

Along its entire length ran the Andes, the world's longest mountain range. Many millions of people lived in that Andean region, a population made up of many different ethnic and linguistic groups. Yet within an incredibly short time, Pizarro and his tiny band of Spaniards would crush Inca resistance, control the government, and take possession of all the Inca lands and treasures.

How did they do it? Why? And what effect did their conquest have upon the course of world history? These are some of the issues this book will try to explain.

O N E

Where Pizarro Came from

To understand what Francisco Pizarro did, we need to know something about where he came from and how he grew up. He was born in the Spanish town of Trujillo around 1475. Spain sits on the Iberian Peninsula, in the southwestern corner of Europe. It shares this peninsula with much-smaller Portugal. Because the peninsula is surrounded on two sides by the Atlantic Ocean and the Mediterranean Sea, most Iberian men naturally became sailors.

Europe in that time was just emerging from the medieval era. It was an agricultural and sparsely settled continent. Spain, for instance, had only about 8 million people. Men and women did not expect to live long; they might reach the age of thirty-five if they were lucky. Life was hard and uncertain. Poor nutrition, lack of medical knowledge, and epidemics of bubonic plague all conspired to cut life short.

The great majority of medieval people lived on scattered farms or

Cadiz, the port in Spain from which many conquistadores sailed to the New World

in small villages. Most were born, married, and died close by their parish church. Historian J. R. Hale estimates that the longest journey made by most people in their lifetime was 15 miles (24 km). Among the relative few who took longer journeys were traders carrying their goods to seasonal markets in the larger cities.

In contrast, the whole royal court of a country would pick up and move from one place to another. The royals, the nobility, the officials, and their staff settled for a time in one palace, then in another. Students, too, were mobile, switching from university to university, building up degrees piecemeal. Pilgrimages to sacred sites sent people, sometimes in the thousands, far from home.

Portrait of the Holy Roman Emperor Charles V,
made by Renaissance artist Titian

But by Pizarro's time ordinary people, too, began roaming the roads looking for work. While Europe's population was growing slowly, there were still more people than farming alone could employ, so a steady stream of men left home to find jobs, above all, as soldiers. Many headed for places where war had broken out and became mercenary troops overnight. What other way could men with no skills better themselves?

There was more than enough fighting to satisfy a man's thirst for blood or his need for work. For centuries the Spanish fought to rid their country of invaders. Back in A.D. 711, the Moors, a Muslim people from North Africa, had crossed to the Iberian Peninsula and occupied most of Spain. In 1492 when Pizarro was about seventeen, they were finally driven out. That year was significant for other reasons, too. The Inquisition in 1492 succeeded in forcibly expelling the Jews from Spain. And with the support of the Spanish rulers, Ferdinand and Isabella, Christopher Columbus set sail across the Atlantic for what he thought would be a new route to the riches of Asia.

Columbus's voyage succeeded in pushing Europe's frontier westward across the ocean. But this was not the first time Europeans had made contact with distant lands. Earlier, crusaders had moved into the Holy Land of the Middle East. Portuguese sailors had landed on the Canary Islands in the Atlantic and moved down the coast of Africa and into Asia. The voyages of exploration following Columbus gradually made Europeans understand that strange new worlds existed.

By the early 1500s, Spain would become the center of one of the greatest empires in world history. But even the Spanish did not know it as the "Spanish Empire." To Europeans it was the Holy Roman Empire. Political alliances among European powers, helped by royal marriages, led to the formation of the Habsburg dynasty. In 1516 Charles V, the grandson of Ferdinand and Isabella and of Maximilian of Habsburg and Marie of Burgundy, became by circumstances (bribery among them)

Holy Roman Emperor. Three dynasties met in him—those of Austria, Burgundy, and Spain. He came into possession of so many portions of Europe that it seemed he owned the whole continent.

To all that would be added the New World—the gift of the conquistadores.

T W O

The Spanish Conquistadores

When Columbus landed on the tiny island of San Salvador in the Caribbean Sea, he thought he had found a new route to Asia. His famous letter reporting his voyage to his Spanish majesties was quickly published and within a year went through twelve editions. It excited everyone interested in overseas trade. His letter was like a sales promotion piece, whipping up the appetite for gold and glory.

Trained as warriors during the civil wars between Christians and Muslims, many Spaniards were ready to risk their lives sailing perilous seas and confronting unknown dangers in strange lands. They were eager to convert natives to Catholicism, and even more eager to get rich quick. Columbus and the conquistadores who followed him presented themselves as soldiers of the Catholic faith and redeemers of souls. With such a self-image, they felt justified, in their obsessive pursuit of gold, to commit atrocities against the native peoples of the Americas.

The Spanish Conquistadores

On his second voyage, Columbus founded a settlement on an island he named Hispaniola in honor of Spain. The island now includes both Haiti and the Dominican Republic. It was the first colony in the New World.

His third voyage brought him to the north coast of South America, and his fourth and last voyage to the mainland of Central America. When he died in 1506, he was still convinced he had reached Asia by sailing west.

Long after the event, an artist imagines
the 1492 landing of Columbus on San Salvador.

A caravel, the type of ship used by the
early explorers of the Americas

The Spanish Conquistadores

Successful passage across the ocean would not have been possible without great advances in shipbuilding, navigation, and astronomy. Portugal led the way. Its ships were the first to sail down the west coast of Africa and out onto the Atlantic to the islands dotting the ocean. Its shipyards developed the caravel, a ship designed not only to carry explorers to new lands, but also to bring them safely home. These discovery ships were not cargo vessels. As the historian Daniel Boorstin put it, their "important cargo was *news*, which could be carried in a small parcel, even in the mind of one man, but which was definitely a return product . . . feedback was the explorer's commodity."

The three ships that sailed on Columbus's first voyage—the *Nina*, the *Pinta*, and the *Santa Maria*—were all of caravel design. The little vessels were long enough to hold a small crew and their supplies. They were only about 70 feet (21 m) in length and about 25 feet (7.6 m) in the beam, and carried two or three lateen sails. They had about three masts—the foremast carried a square sail, and the others carried triangular lateen sails. With a shallow draft, they could explore inshore waters and easily be beached for careening, or repairs. The reputation they quickly gained for safety on long round trips made it easier to recruit seamen for voyages of discovery.

Exploration of the New World continued, dominated by Spain and Portugal. In 1497 and 1499, Amerigo Vespucci, an Italian sailing for Spain, passed along the north and east coasts of South America. In 1500 a Spanish navigator, Vicente Pinzón, touched the coast of Brazil and reached the mouth of the Amazon River. A few months later a Portuguese navigator, Pedro Álvars Cabral, reached the southern part of Brazil.

In 1508 Spaniards came upon the Yucatán, in Central America, thinking it was probably an island. Juan Ponce de León, who had helped drive the Moors out of Spain and accompanied Columbus on his second voyage, took over what is now known as Puerto Rico, enriching himself with gold, slaves, and land. In 1513, he sailed northeast from Puerto Rico and landed on the peninsula that came to be called Florida.

That same year, the Spanish conquistador Vasco Núñez de Balboa slashed through the tropical forest of the Isthmus of Panama and discovered the Pacific Ocean on its western shore. He promptly claimed it for the Spanish crown.

Hernán Cortés (along with Pizarro, the most famous of the Spanish conquistadores) sailed to Mexico in 1519 in the hope of acquiring wealth. He penetrated the Aztec Empire; took its ruler, Montezuma, as a hostage; and finally, in 1521, succeeded in overthrowing the capital city, Tenochtitlán—an event that signaled the beginning of 300 years of colonial domination.

The meeting in Mexico of the Spanish conquistador Cortés and the Aztec ruler, Montezuma

The Spanish Conquistadores

By this time, Europeans had realized that a huge landmass stood between their continent and Asia. The great achievement of the Portuguese navigator Ferdinand Magellan in circumnavigating the globe between 1519 and 1521 left no doubt about it. Almost nothing, however, was known about the Pacific coast of South America. The world of the Inca had yet to be entered.

T H R E E

The Business of Conquest

Francisco Pizarro was the son of an infantry officer, Captain Gonzalo Pizarro, and a woman the captain never married. Pizarro was born in Trujillo, a town in the Estremadura, the same region of Spain from which his distant cousin Hernán Cortés came. Little is known of his childhood, except that he never learned to read. But although illiterate, like many Spaniards of his time, he proved to have a mind for business and a powerful will to govern others.

Trujillo would play a role in the conquest of Peru. Of the Europeans who would take part in the capture of the Inca emperor, at least seventeen were from Pizarro's town. It sat atop a hill and was surrounded by a wall. It was the economic center for the surrounding farms, villages, and workshops. Peasants and artisans lived on the outskirts, which also contained the Jewish quarter. On the hilltop were the turreted homes of the knights and members of the lesser nobility, known as Hidalgos.

A portrait of Francisco Pizarro painted about 300 years
after his death

The Pizarros boasted one of the oldest family names in the region, dating back to the thirteenth century. Captain Pizarro was a man with some prestige, but only a small estate. When he died in combat in 1521, a draft of his will showed that he had fathered children by several different women besides the three with his lawful wife. Investigation of the family history indicated Pizarro's mother was Francisca Gonzáles, a servant in a nearby convent. She was the daughter of peasants, and later married someone else. Francisco probably split his early years between his father's and his mother's homes. Pizarro had several half brothers, three of whom would join in the conquest of Peru. It was said of the Pizarros that they were as proud as they were poor.

We do not know what Francisco did or thought in the years he was growing up. The young Pizarro was said to have served as a soldier in Italy. His first recorded act, however, was to sail to the West Indies in 1502 in the fleet of Nicholás de Ovando, the governor of Hispaniola. Already about twenty-six years old—which was considered quite old for that time—he might have been planning to become rich on the island estate of his uncle, Juan Pizarro. But there is no record of that. Over the next few years, he took part in at least two exploratory ventures on the islands. From these expeditions, wrote a Spaniard who knew him, he and his comrades returned "with many Indians and slaves, and very good gold, and they also used their cruelties on the Indians, for this evil habit was much used, and Pizarro knew it by heart, having used it for years before."

In 1513, when Balboa and his conquistadores came across the Pacific on the far side of Panama, Pizarro was one of his senior officers. He stayed on when Spain established a permanent colony in Panama. Gradually he acquired farms and Indian slaves to run them. He added to his prosperity as part owner of a gold mine the Indians had led them to.

The Business of Conquest

The Spanish in Panama had begun to explore the northwest coast of South America, excited by stories of a land to the south rumored to be fabulously rich in gold. "Birú" or "Peru," it was called.

Acting under orders from the governor of Panama, Pizarro's troops abruptly seized Balboa while he was preparing an expedition to Peru. Balboa was falsely accused of disloyalty to the Spanish crown and of planning to set himself up as emperor of Peru. Pizarro had Balboa and four companions beheaded in the public square and their bodies thrown to the vultures.

Now wealthy, Pizarro could have returned to his hometown and lived a pleasant life, like a nobleman. But his greed for more gold knew no limit. Why shouldn't he be the one to find Peru and make it into his

A twentieth-century artist imagines Balboa viewing the Pacific Ocean in 1513.

own kingdom? Like other enterprising Europeans, he was tantalized by the huge financial returns made in Mexico, which Cortés had conquered. Merchants and bankers used to investing in trade, in plantations, and in mining were eagerly putting money into the conquest of more new territories.

Exploration and conquest were approached much like a business venture. Spaniards would set up an expedition, each partner responsible for his own equipment and weapons. In return, whatever their journey produced in the way of land or loot, each would receive a set share of the profits, but no salary. Only the sailors were paid wages.

The earliest expeditions in the West Indies hunted for gold, spices, pearls, and slaves. When explorers found they lacked the capital to overcome the great risks, they began to entice more investors. The new investors came not only from Spain, but also from other countries of Europe. They counted on the conquest companies to take complete control of the native peoples, so that permanent settlements could be established and they could reap the profits of their investments.

Although Pizarro was and would remain illiterate, he understood the ways of the business world and was confident he would enrich himself and his investors.

At age forty, Pizarro was one of the most experienced veterans of Spain's expanding empire. He had gone through many tests of his courage and leadership, and mastered the technical and political skills needed to stay on top in a cutthroat world.

The conquest of Peru would challenge his military talents. To advance Spain's empire beyond the Caribbean and Mexico would demand a higher price than he had ever before paid.

F O U R

A Glimpse of Gold

It was in the fall of 1524 that Pizarro took his first step toward Peru. With him was his business partner Diego de Almagro. Veterans of the West Indies, they had every expectation of quick success. Their ship carried eighty men and four horses. They had scarcely gone below the Isthmus of Panama when they met trouble. Almagro lost an eye in a skirmish with the Indians, and mangrove swamps infested with insects ruined their plan to establish settlements. Their hopes of finding great wealth were also dashed, though they did collect a few pieces of gold.

Although disappointed, Pizarro and Almagro took a third partner, Hernando de Luque, a priest. Early in 1526 the three men embarked on a bigger venture, carrying 160 men and several horses on two small ships commanded by the pilot Bartolomé Ruiz, who had invested some gold pieces in the enterprise. Reaching the San Juan River in Colombia, the

Diego de Almagro—Pizarro's business partner

partners separated. Pizarro pitched camp there, Almagro returned to Panama for reinforcements, and Ruiz sailed south.

It was Ruiz, crossing the equator in the Pacific, who suddenly saw the first sign of the Inca civilization. He spotted a large balsa-wood trading raft fitted with a triangular cotton sail floating toward them. Aboard the raft were twenty crew members and passengers. As the Spaniards set about capturing them, eleven jumped into the sea to escape. What dazzled the Spaniards? They described it in a report sent to Charles V, the Holy Roman Emperor.

They were carrying many pieces of silver and gold as personal ornaments . . . including crowns and diadems, belts and bracelets, armour for the legs and breastplates, tweezers and rattles and strings and clusters of beads and rubies; mirrors decorated with silver, and cups and other drinking vessels. They were carrying many wool and cotton mantles and Moorish tunics . . . and other pieces of clothing coloured with cochineal, crimson, blue, yellow and all other colours, and worked with different types of ornate embroidery, in figures of birds, animals, fish and trees. They had some tiny weights to weight gold . . . There were small stones in bead bags; emeralds and chalcedonies and other jewels and pieces of crystal and resin. They were taking all this to trade for fish shells from which they make counters [a kind of coin], *coral-coloured scarlet and white.*

When the Spaniards reached shore, they set six of the Indians free. Ruiz held two others, planning to have them taught Spanish so that they could serve as interpreters during the conquest of the new lands they would discover.

Using sign language, the captives told Ruiz that the raft's mission was to barter Inca artifacts for other goods. Their gold came from a distant land in the south.

A Glimpse of Gold

Ruiz brought his captives and the trade goods to Pizarro. The expedition then moved south to explore the coast of what is now called Ecuador. They landed on Gallo, an uninhabited island in a river estuary. It proved to be a poor choice. The heat was terrible, and no crops could grow in the poisonous mangrove swamps. Three or four men died of hunger and disease every week. The vision of a golden fortune raised by the raft's crew faded. Mutiny threatened.

As their numbers dwindled, Ruiz's ship left Ecuador. One of the men smuggled himself out to Panama and appealed to the governor for help, charging that Pizarro was crazed. The governor of Panama sent back an order that any man who wanted out should be allowed to leave. That none had left thus far was a mark of Pizarro's grim determination to keep the expedition going at all costs.

A rescue mission was sent in late August 1527. When the boat arrived, Pizarro staged a dramatic scene. With his sword he drew a

A balsa-wood raft, used on trading voyages by the Inca people

line in the sand, and said, "Comrades and friends, on that side lies the part which represented death, hardship, hunger, nakedness and abandonment; this side here represents comfort. Here you return to Panama—to be poor! There you may go to Peru—to be rich. You choose which best becomes you as brave Spaniards."

Later, the historian Ciezo de León talked to some of the men who had been on that beach. They said most of them ignored Pizarro's appeal. They had had more than enough of so miserable a life. Only thirteen out of some eighty men stayed. The rescue ship's captain agreed to carry Pizarro and his thirteen loyalists to another island called Gorgona. He left them some maize rations and the two Indians Ruiz had hoped to train as interpreters. But he refused to let them have a small boat.

In effect, they were marooned on an island 6 miles (9.6 km) long, hot, humid, and with unrelenting rainfall. Luckily, they found lots of small animals—monkeys, lizards, birds, and turtles. Here they could survive, and under Pizarro's leadership they did, for seven long months. But as time dragged by, they began to believe they would die on the lonely island. Then, late in March 1528, someone spied a ship on the horizon. It was Ruiz, sailing from Panama under orders from Almagro, Pizarro's other partner.

Almost hopeless until the moment the ship was sighted, Pizarro was overjoyed at the prospect of pushing deeper south, toward Peru. Others would surely have wished to return to Panama for rest and security. But not Pizarro. With Ruiz, the Indian interpreters, and his thirteen loyalists he sailed down the coast of Colombia and Ecuador until, after some three weeks at sea, the Indians spotted their home on the coast. It was the town of Tumbes. The people on shore were amazed at the sight of such a strange ship. But they were not frightened. They jumped aboard their balsa-wood rafts and sailed out to greet the newcomers.

A Glimpse of Gold

It was a historic first exchange between the Inca people and Europeans. Eyewitness reports of the Inca interpreters tell us what happened between Pizarro and the Inca noble who came aboard.

He asked the captain where were they from, what land they had come from, and what were they looking for, or what was their purpose in going by sea and land without stopping? Francisco Pizarro replied that they had come from Spain, where they were native, and that in that land there was a great and powerful king called Charles, whose vassal and servants they were, and many others because he ruled wide territories. They had left their land to explore these parts, as they could see, and to place what they found under the king's authority, but primarily, and above all, to let them know that the

A Spanish priest attempts to convert the Inca people to Christianity.

idols they worshipped were false, and that to save their souls they had to become Christians and believe in the God the Spanish worshipped, who was in heaven, because those who did not worship him would go to hell, a dark place and full of fire. Those who know the truth and take him as God, the only lord of Creation, will live in heaven forever.

Did the Inca leader understand this terrible threat? Was it translated into Quechua, his language? Pizarro was carrying out what was now almost a routine formality. He was reciting the Requirement, a document issued in 1493 by Pope Alexander VI, telling foreign powers that their land was now Spain's, by order of the pope.

The Inca leader invited the Spanish to come ashore to share their food and take whatever else they might need, "without fear of harm." Inca eyewitnesses told the historian León that each side took the other to be "rational" people. The Spanish were astonished that the Inca chief seemed so civilized.

When the Spaniards went ashore and walked around Tumbes, they saw fine buildings, cultivated fields, and irrigation canals. It was the northernmost coastal city of the Inca Empire. Beautiful women came up and communicated with them in sign language. These welcoming strangers, and the sight of gold on Inca temple walls, made the Spanish marvel that these pagans seemed to be so civilized.

Just this glimpse of Peru and its wealth was enough to convince Pizarro to return to Spain to seek a royal license for the conquest of the Inca Empire. It took more time than expected. But in July 1529 he won the support of the crown and investors and recruited the volunteers needed for his attack force. In 1530 he was back in Panama, and in December he sailed again to Peru. With him were his three brothers—Gonzalo, Hernando, and Juan—his partners, and two hundred men.

FIVE

The Inca Empire

When Pizarro led his expedition toward the land of the Inca, he had no notion of its size, its population, its culture, or its history. Research by historians and archeologists today has uncovered many facts. We now know what Pizarro confronted.

The land occupied by the Inca Empire was much larger than today's Republic of Peru. It covered most of modern Peru, Bolivia, and Ecuador, as well as parts of Colombia, Chile, and Argentina. Such a huge territory is marked by great contrasts of climate and terrain. The immense Pacific Ocean lay off its western shore. Bordering it were coastal deserts cut by lush areas watered by rivers draining from the Andes. To the east were the semitropical rain forests of the Amazon. Between these extremes rose the high plateaus and lofty peaks of the snowcapped Andes Mountains.

Pizarro's expedition climbing the high peaks of the Andes to reach the heart of the Inca Empire

Evidence of human habitation of the Andean highlands goes back at least 13,000 years. The ancestors of these earliest inhabitants had migrated from Siberia to North America across a land bridge that existed during the last Ice Age. They were hunters and gatherers, but over the next several million years they turned to agriculture. They domesticated chiefly three different animals. Llamas were used for meat and for transporting burdens. They also made use of alpacas, a closely related species, which provided wool so fine that it was spun and woven into textiles. The guinea pig was raised as well and was a source of meat.

The Inca formed the largest pre-Hispanic empire in the Americas. The empire's limits were set partly by nature and partly by the resistance of non-Inca groups who opposed being absorbed. The Inca Empire was only one century old at the time Pizarro entered. Called Tawantinsuyu—Land of the Four Parts—it embraced more than one hundred societies, the Inca people among them.

The Four Parts referred to the empire's four sections: northeast, northwest, southeast, and southwest. Each quarter had its own governor, and within each quarter were several provinces, administered by ethnic Inca or local elites. According to varying estimates, the empire included some 6 million to 15 million people living under the authority of the Inca king.

Pizarro found the Incas to be superstitious. In this painting by Giulio Ferrario, the Incas are awed by a lunar eclipse.

Everyone had to work, even little children. If you did not till the soil, you worked as a craftsperson or in some other specialized field. Everyone had a job to do. Quitting or loafing brought stiff punishment. Even the nobility were part of the economic system. The nobles were assigned the loftier functions of high priests, ambassadors, governors, and military commanders. At the topmost level were the princes, descended from the Inca royal family. To this rank the Inca added the loyal chiefs of conquered tribes.

Inca society had no middle class of landowners and merchants. The emperor, who owned everything, divided the animals and the land into three portions. One part was set aside for his own use. Another supported the temples, priests, and attendants of the state religion. And the third was parceled out among the empire's people. What you received was based on the number of people in your family.

The elite, those of high status, were relieved from labor duty. They had their lands and herds tended for them and received household service. The elite were set apart by dress, furniture, and diet—including the right to get high by chewing the coca leaf, a stimulant. The plant was grown for its "magical" powers. It had a role in the Inca religion and was often scattered or burned as an offering to the gods. When leaves of

A coca bag decorated with a llama pattern

the plant were chewed and mixed with lime or potash, narcotic substances were released that suppressed hunger, thirst, and fatigue. Ordinary people contrived to get their share of that substance. They needed it to carry out the most burdensome labor. But they took coca for pure pleasure, too, hoping to avoid punishment if informers or inspectors spotted them.

Artisans who worked for the state made fine wool tapestries, feathered textiles, metal and wooden goods, and ceramics (painted with colorful designs) as well as other products. Some people specialized in household service, administration, and other occupations.

Religion in the Andean region was not uniform. The locally based tribal groups had their own beliefs and practices. These varied from place to place, paying homage to local earth, mountain, and water spirits and deities. Inca religion embraced the beliefs and ritual practices of the Inca nobility, promoted through the priesthood and political agents, for the benefit of the Inca state. The driving goal behind the Inca religion was to unify all the local groups within the empire in the service of the Incas.

At the heart of the Inca religion and government was the city of Cuzco, in present-day south-central Peru. The ruling Inca was believed to be a descendant and earthly manifestation of the Sun. The Inca queen was linked to the Moon. The nobility were related to the Inca king or were close descendants of past rulers.

The Incas built temples of the Sun in Cuzco and in other major administrative centers of the empire. There were hundreds of sacred sites in the empire—such as buildings, carved rocks, and springs. Each received sacrificial offerings—such as shells and coca leaves—on particular days in the Inca ritual calendar. On certain special occasions, human victims—including children—were selected in the provinces and were sacrificed to seal a bond between the Inca in Cuzco and the provincial nobility. As the Inca Empire expanded, its religion absorbed local tribal deities and objects of worship. (And later, in the Spanish colonial era, that tradition continued with the blending of Catholicism and the Inca religion.) Religion for the common people of Peru, says the historian John Hemming, meant a

> *world of spirits and superstition. Almost any circumstance—a double ear of maize, a dream, an accident—represented a supernatural manifestation. Each village was surrounded by a mass of*

An Inca priest

THE INCA

Inca is loosely translated as "king" or "emperor." It is often mistakenly applied to all the ancient Peruvians. In Quechua, the Inca language, its meaning is "archetype," or "perfect example." The Inca ruler was the Unique Inca—*the* Inca. Other ancient emperors, too, in China, Japan, and Egypt for example, were held to be a son of heaven or a child of the Sun.

An Inca ruler holding aloft the symbol of the Sun

huacas (sacred places): trees, springs, rocks, caves that had magical significance. Each house had its canopas or household deities, some object displayed in a niche in the wall or carefully wrapped in cloths. The Indians collected talismans of unusual objects, like modern schoolboys. They observed propitiary [pacifying] rituals throughout their daily lives, sprinkling chicha or coca when ploughing, saying prayers when crossing rivers, making sacrifices at appropriate occasions, and always leaving an object on the pile of stones still to be found at the top of every pass. They lived in awe of their sorcerers, the old men who foretold the future by studying the entrails of animals or the clouds, and were terrified of black magic, spells that could induce pain or love in selected victims. The Incas themselves, for all their sophistication, shared these fears.

An Inca temple of the Sun at Cuzco

Perhaps most astonishing to the Spanish invaders would be the fact that the Incas seemed to have no concept of private property, except that everything seemed to belong to the emperor. Recent research, however, suggests that land grants were made as rewards to nobles and military leaders. The ordinary people, the peasants, had no horses, mules, or oxen to help with their farming or transport. The men worked the earth with foot plows, while the women broke the sod, hoed, and planted. Maize, beans, potatoes, and quinoa were the important crops.

The potato, cultivated as early as 5000 B.C.E., was the staple food in the highlands, where maize would not grow. It came in many sizes, shapes, and colors. The Inca knew not only how to grow the potato, but also how to preserve it. They created probably the world's first

A human sacrifice was an occasional ritual of the Inca religion.

freeze-dried food, calling it by the Inca name, *chuño*. They bartered *chuño* for other foods, carrying it on the backs of llamas to the lower valleys and coastal towns, where it was exchanged for maize and manioc, clay pottery, and woven cloths.

Pottery depicting a parrot eating maize, a staple Inca crop

The power of the Inca state was built upon a labor tax. Economic life was organized around the household. Each married man and his household made up a tribute-paying unit. Such units were combined into groups under the direction of either Inca or local leaders. These leaders would assign units to carry out a great many kinds of labor. These included farming, herding, brewing maize beer, construction, weaving, mining, guard duty, and military service.

The provincial centers the empire was built upon were connected by more than 2,000 way stations, linked by 25,000 miles (40,232 km) of serviced roads. Like other Native Americans, the Inca had no wheeled vehicles. People walked to where they had to go. Professional porters carried the heavy loads. The upper class—kings, queens, nobles—were carried in litters or sedan chairs. Llamas were mustered, sometimes in the thousands, for pack trains. They crisscrossed the empire, bearing products from one climate zone to another, bringing campaigning troops food and equipment and carrying farm produce or craft goods to state storage centers.

The highway system was made up of two main north-south routes, one running along the coast, the other through the Andes Mountains.

Inca ingenuity achieved such wonders as this hanging bridge.

Roads running east to west connected the coast and highland roads. In addition, minor roads and trails linked small towns, villages, and hamlets into the main highway system. In the mountain region, Inca engineers had to build tunnels and bridges, some out of great slabs of rock, others out of tree trunks cut down in the jungle.

Many of the highways had been built by earlier peoples, but the Inca connected the disjointed segments into an integrated system. Work needed on the highways was carried out by the local communities, as part of their labor tax. Along the routes were state rest centers for the use of officials, porters, and troops, as well as stations for the messenger service, manned usually by one or two young men who were trained from an early age to do this work. They memorized messages and carried them quickly in relays from one station to the next. Distances between these post houses ran from a half mile (0.8 km) to 5 miles (8 km). The runners' speed was remarkable. However, they relied on more than their own muscle. They chewed the coca leaf, which helped them ignore their discomforts. At each station were sleeping shelters and places for storage of food and goods. The unique highway system connected the Inca Empire into a single network for communication and administration. "The roads," said the archeologist William Isbell, "were at once the vehicle and symbol of Inca power."

Yet, with the roads and almost every other kind of work carried out by a system of forced labor, it was a culture, writes historian David S. Landes, that "deprived the ordinary person of initiative, autonomy, and personality."

Even more impressive than the highway system was Inca architecture. Many buildings were constructed of fine-cut stone and mortarless masonry. Others combined fieldstone and mud-brick walls. Coastal centers were built of adobe. For garrisons and gatherings in provincial centers there were large, single-room structures.

The quipu was a recording device made of a series of colored and knotted strings. "Keepers of the quipu" recorded such details as numbers of llamas, quantities of farm products, and historical events.

Groups of people lived in rectangular enclosures, gabled houses facing onto patios.

The language of the Incas was Quechua. Although only one of many languages spoken by the various tribal and ethnic groups in the vast region, it was imposed throughout the empire for control and unification purposes. It prevailed over all others, and today more than half the people of Peru speak it as their first language.

While the Peruvians displayed their talents in many fields, they never developed the equivalent to the Western system of writing. To record numerical data or historical events, they used the *quipu*. The quipu was a row of knotted strings in which the color of the threads and the loops and positions of the knots represented numbers or other kinds of records, such as historical events. A complex color scheme and arrangement of knots made for an effective mnemonic (memory) aid. Quipus, ceramics, and textiles, such as woven blankets and tunics, were also developed as record-keeping devices. They are highly rated, too, as examples of ancient Andean art. In addition, there were official narrative poems praising the deeds of each Inca ruler that were memorized and recited by professional attendants.

By military power, making alliances, spreading their Quechua language, imposing a unifying state religion, reorganizing the territory, developing an administrative bureaucracy, and negotiating agreements, the Inca built their empire. Their skill in governing enabled them to administer the activities of a great variety of ethnic groups speaking their own languages, dwelling in different environments, and cherishing their own ethnic traditions.

It was this civilization that Pizarro was to invade in May 1532.

SIX

Epidemics and Civil Wars

When Pizarro's expedition landed in northern Peru, he found the Inca state shaken by two powerful forces—the devastation of European diseases and civil war among the Inca nobility itself.

Disease is a major reason why the native peoples of the Americas were so vulnerable to European invaders. Before the arrival of Columbus in 1492, measles, influenza, smallpox, yellow fever, cholera, malaria, and bubonic plague were unknown in the New World. They had not, for whatever reason, migrated along with the early people who crossed from Siberia to North America in the last Ice Age.

The Native Americans had diseases of their own, but relatively few, and not so deadly. The historian Ronald Wright estimates that "Old World plagues killed at least half the population of the Aztec, Maya, and Inca civilizations shortly before their overthrow. The sheer loss of

Pizarro's Routes
1524-1532

CARIBBEAN SEA

Nombre de Dios

Panama

VENEZUELA

COLOMBIA

Atacames

Equator

ECUADOR

Cuenca

Tumbes

San Miguel

BRAZIL

Cajamarca

PERU

Lima

Machu Picchu

Cuzco

ANDES MOUNTAINS

PACIFIC

OCEAN

CHILE

ATLANTIC

OCEAN

SOUTH

AMERICA

Inca
Empire

0   300   600mi

Pizarro & Almagro 1524
Pizarro & Almagro 1526
First relief ship 1526
Second relief ship 1527
Third expedition 1532

people was devastating enough . . . but disease was also a political assassination squad, removing kings, generals, and seasoned advisers at the very time they were needed most."

Among the many killed was Huayna Capac, the Inca ruler who had held the throne since 1493. Reports described him as a short man, "but strong and well-made, with a fine face and grave expression; a man of few words and many deeds." He was esteemed as "a great friend of the poor, who ordered that they should be given special care throughout the land."

News of invaders came to the Inca leader late in 1527, when couriers reported that strange, bearded, pale-skinned men had landed on the island of Gallo. With the Spanish came the plague of smallpox. The disease had already taken its huge toll among the Aztecs and the Maya, and may have been carried farther south by Pizarro's expedition. Or it could have spread overland, through Panama and Colombia, and then attacked Huayna Capac's people. As it had done in Central America, smallpox killed at least half the Inca Empire's population, and much of its leadership. The Inca emperor was a victim, and so was his son and heir.

As he lay dying, Huayna warned his children and his governors that an invasion from beyond their empire was coming, and that they should prepare to resist it.

But the ruling group faced more than an outside enemy and disease. For as the Inca people expanded their empire over many decades, not every tribe submitted to their control. Some hated giving up their land, and mourned the loss of those captured or killed. They also resented having to pay the fixed labor tribute. Those who rebelled openly were treated with ruthless cruelty.

One by one, however, the many tribes in the north and south fell to the Inca, losing their independence. In so vast an empire, total control was difficult, almost impossible. As far back as 1493, when Huayna

Atahualpa,
Huayna Capac's son

Capac inherited the throne, the empire had been seething with revolt. Military action to put down the rebels had cost the Inca emperor some of his best troops. Discontent even reached into the emperor's personal regiments of Inca nobles.

Nevertheless, it seems Huayna Capac was esteemed by most as an experienced leader. Had the Inca Empire not lost him at this moment, the outcome of Pizarro's invasion might have been different. With his death, however, the empire was torn apart by wars between two of his surviving sons, each claiming the throne. That struggle for power not only split the Inca royalty at the moment when unity was so vital, but also gave unhappy subjects the chance to revolt against Inca domination.

47

Aside from finding riches, one of Pizarro's main goals in Peru
was to spread Christianity. Here, a missionary priest addresses
Atahualpa during Pizarro's conquest.

Objective circumstances could not have been better for Pizarro. As noted above, he had entered Tumbes once before, in 1528, had then returned to Panama, and from there had taken a ship to Spain, where he obtained royal approval and backers. He sailed back to Panama with a small fleet bearing volunteers who included his half brothers, Hernando, Juan, and Gonzalo. This, comments historian Michael Wood, marked the beginning of the family's "almost Mafia-like grip on the affairs of Peru." As an entrepreneurial organization, it would grow into

WHAT HAPPENED TO THE HORSE?

The modern horse evolved millions of years ago. It spread from the plains of North America to South America and across the land bridge from Alaska to Siberia and all parts of Europe and Asia. Then a strange thing happened. For millions of years the horse thrived in its American homeland. Then, about 10,000 years ago, it disappeared from the Americas. No one is sure of the reason. Not until the ships of the Spanish explorers carried them to the New World 500 years ago did horses return to their native land. They arrived on the ships of Columbus, Ponce de León, and Hernán Cortés. Pizarro introduced horses to the Inca Empire.

an immense enterprise, with the private interests of the Pizarros linked to the political aims of the Spanish empire.

In May 1532 Pizarro sailed again into Tumbes—the coastal town in the north—with a small expeditionary force. However, he found Tumbes reduced to ruins by the fighting between Huayna Capac's sons, Atahualpa and Huascar. Pizarro sensed that he could make use of the conflict. A divided society would be easier to break apart. So he moved south, setting up a community in a fertile valley. He promptly enslaved those Indians who had not fled and set them to work building a Spanish settlement.

So few invaders? How could the Spanish expect to conquer the vast Inca Empire and its millions of people?

For one thing the Spaniards had confidence in the superiority of their weapons. Pizarro had already spent years in the New World and knew what its limited weaponry was like. The Spaniards had guns; the Native Americans had none. But in those times guns—called harquebuses—were hard to load and fire, and Pizarro had only a dozen of them. The Inca fought with slings (to hurl egg-size stones), javelins, bolas (thrown to entangle an enemy's legs), spiked maces, and war clubs with star-shaped heads.

Such weapons were not very effective against the Spaniards' steel armor and steel helmets, their swords, lances, harquebuses, and crossbows. But the greatest advantage was given by the Spaniards' horses. Horses were unknown in the New World at that time. The Peruvians, who had never seen either white people or horses, were amazed at the strange spectacle. Some thought these men in armor astride horses were a new kind of beast—dragons or centaurs (half men, half beasts). Others were appalled to hear that deer bearing strange beings on their backs "as high as rooftops" were coming to attack them. They were told that the horses could catch anyone whom they ran after and that the guns could kill from a distance.

The Spaniards would take advantage of the Inca's shock and would deliver a message to the Inca leaders. Once again they would represent themselves as instruments of His Holiness, the pope, who held divine power and who had sent the Spaniards to rule the earth.

SEVEN

The Decisive Day

November 16, 1532, was the decisive day.

It marked the first encounter between the Inca emperor Atahualpa and the Spanish conquistador Francisco Pizarro. The place was Cajamarca, a town in the Peruvian highlands.

The Inca was absolute monarch of the largest and most advanced state in the Americas. Pizarro represented the Holy Roman Emperor Charles V, monarch of the most powerful state in Europe.

With Pizarro was his "army" of 164 soldiers—62 men on horses and 102 on foot. Thirty-eight were rated gentlemen, and a third of the total, like their leader, were illiterate. With them were the Quechua-speaking prisoners Pizarro had taken on this second voyage. Now that these interpreters were fluent in Spanish, Pizarro could communicate.

Atahualpa was in the heart of his own empire of many millions and at the head of an army of 80,000 army veterans.

Pizarro and the Inca leader Atahualpa meet at Cajamarca.

We know from several eyewitnesses what happened. Six of Pizarro's men wrote accounts that have come down to us.

As he marched into the Inca Empire from its northern end, Pizarro, through his interpreters, learned that the civil war between Atahualpa and his brother Huascar was getting hotter and hotter. He knew Cortés had taken advantage of the internal conflict among the Aztecs of Mexico to conquer that empire. Couldn't he do the same?

It was a trying journey up and down the freezing Andean highlands. The dizzying altitudes and the bitter cold sickened some of the men. They were frightened too. They couldn't count on reinforcements, for the nearest Spaniards were 1,000 miles (1,609 km) away. Would they be trapped in a mountain pass? What cruelties would they suffer if captured by strange warriors? But Pizarro's iron will forced them on.

The Decisive Day

Finally, late on November 14, 1532, the Spaniards reached the outskirts of Cajamarca. Standing above the town, they could see a sprawling military camp and the smoke spiraling up from thousands of fires. It was Atahualpa's army—a "fearful sight." How many warriors were there? They estimated 30,000, but the truth was more like 80,000.

Not long before, Atahualpa's troops had ambushed the forces of his brother Huascar and taken Huascar prisoner. When Atahualpa got the news, he ordered his officers to kill Huascar's family. As Huascar was made to watch, his whole family—wives, children, brothers, sisters—was slaughtered. And then all his known followers were dragged from their houses and killed.

By the time Pizarro confronted Atahualpa, tens of thousands of the empire's fighting men had been killed in the civil war.

At the center of Cajamarca was a great public square, used for civic and religious ceremonies and as a parade ground for the military. Word had reached Atahualpa of the Spaniards' ruthless behavior. He probably meant to capture and kill them. But out of curiosity and a lack of fear, he decided to meet them in the town square.

The Spaniards were full of fear because they saw how vastly outnumbered they were. That night they talked for hours, planning what to do the next day. In the morning a messenger came from Atahualpa. Pizarro told him, "Let your lord come meet me whenever and wherever he may choose. I will receive him as a friend and brother. No harm or insult will befall him."

What happened next has come down to us in the words of the Spaniards who recorded the events of November 16, 1532. It is our only record, for the Inca left none.

The passages quoted are excerpts from eyewitness accounts by six of Pizarro's companions, including his brothers.

The killing of Huascar by order of his half brother, Atahualpa

The Decisive Day

The Governor [Pizarro] concealed his troops around the square at Cajamarca, dividing the cavalry into two portions of which he gave the command of one to his brother Hernando Pizarro and the command of the other to Hernando de Soto. In like manner he divided the infantry, he himself taking one part and giving the other to his brother Juan Pizarro. At the same time, he ordered Pedro de Candia with two or three infantrymen to go with trumpets to a small fort in the plaza and to station themselves there with a small piece of artillery. When all the Indians, and Atahualpa with them, had entered the Plaza, the Governor would give a signal to Candia and his men, after which they should start firing the gun, and the trumpets should sound, and at the sound of the trumpets the cavalry should dash out of the large court where they were waiting hidden in readiness.

At noon Atahualpa, accompanied by thousands of Indian warriors, together with high lords and military chiefs, entered the plaza.

Governor Pizarro now sent Friar Vicente de Valverde to go speak to Atahualpa, and to require Atahualpa in the name of God and of the King of Spain that Atahualpa subject himself to the law of our Lord Jesus Christ and to the service of His Majesty the King of Spain. Advancing with a cross in one hand and the Bible in the other hand, and going among the Indian troops up to the place where Atahualpa was, the Friar thus addressed him: "I am a Priest of God, and I teach Christians the things of God, and in like manner I come to teach you. What I teach is that which God says to us in this Book. Therefore, on the part of God and of the Christians, I beseech you to be their friend, for such is God's will, and it will be for your good."

Atahualpa asked for the Book, that he might look at it, and the Friar gave it to him closed. Atahualpa did not know how to open the Book, and the Friar was extending his arm to do so, when

The Decisive Day

Atahualpa, in great anger, gave him a blow on the arm, not wishing that it should be opened. Then he opened it himself, and, without any astonishment at the letters and paper he threw it away from him five or six paces, his face a deep crimson.

The Friar returned to Pizarro, shouting, "Come out! Come out, Christians! Come at these enemy dogs who reject the things of God. That tyrant has thrown my book of holy law to the ground! Did you not see what happened? Why remain polite and servile toward this over-proud dog when the plains are full of Indians? March out against him for I absolve you!"

Pizarro's men seize Atahualpa—a painting by the British artist John Everett Millais made in 1845

The Governor then gave the signal to Candia, who began to fire off the guns. At the same time the trumpets were sounded, and the armored Spanish troops, both cavalry and infantry, sallied forth out of their hiding places straight into the mass of unarmed Indians crowding the square, giving the Spanish battle cry, "Santiago!" We had placed rattles on the horses to terrify the Indians. The booming of the guns, the blowing of the trumpets, and the rattles on the horses threw the Indians into panicked confusion. The Spaniards fell upon them and began to cut them to pieces.

The Spaniards killed about 7,000 Indians and gravely wounded more. The casualties included many Indians of high rank in the empire. As for the emperor himself:

Atahualpa's robes had been torn off when the Spaniards pulled him out of his litter. The Governor ordered clothes to be brought to him, and when Atahualpa was dressed, the Governor ordered Atahualpa to sit near him and soothed his rage and agitation at finding himself so quickly fallen from his high estate. The Governor said to Atahualpa, "Do not take it as an insult that you have been defeated and taken prisoner, for with the Christians who come with me, though so few in number, I have conquered greater kingdoms than yours, and have defeated other more powerful lords than you, imposing upon them the dominion of the Emperor, whose vassal I am, and who is King of Spain and of the universal world. We come to conquer this land by his command, that all may come to a knowledge of God and of His Holy Catholic Faith; and by reason of our good mission, God, the Creator of heaven and earth and of all things in them, permits this, in order that you may know Him and come out from the bestial and diabolical life that you lead. It is for this reason that we, being so few in number, subjugate that vast host. When you have seen the errors in which you live, you will understand the good that we have done you by coming to your land by order of his Majesty the King of Spain. Our Lord permitted that your pride should be brought low and that no Indian should be able to offend a Christian."

EIGHT

Turning an Empire into a Colony

It was an astonishing feat. In one day Pizarro had seized control of the Inca Empire. Atahualpa couldn't believe that so tiny a force meant to take over the empire he himself had just won after a fierce civil war. He thought it more likely that the Spanish were just bandits who could be paid off in gold and then killed on their way out. So he got word out to his generals not to attack the invaders.

The ransom was to be enough gold to fill a palace room 22 feet (6.7 m) long by 17 feet (1.5 m) high, to a width of 8 feet (2.4 m). The Inca ruler sent messengers throughout the land to bring gold to him. Porters and llamas flocked in, carrying vases, bowls, religious figures, ornaments—all made of gold. Pizarro saw only gleaming gold, not beautiful craftsmanship. He had Indian goldsmiths melt down the fruit of centuries of Native American culture into ingots of standard size so that the gold could be divided and carried back to Spain. The

This color lithograph shows Pizarro's men burning Atahualpa to death.
However, historical facts show that the Inca ruler was strangled.

total weight came to 13,265 pounds (6,017 kg) of gold and 26,000 pounds (11,793.6 kg) of silver. The value by today's standards was probably more than $50 million. The value in lost art objects is beyond measure.

Eight months later, with the ransom fully paid, it was time to release Atahualpa. Pizarro, fearing that Atahualpa was plotting to kill him and expel the Spaniards, broke his pledge and, on July 26, 1533, had Atahualpa strangled in a public execution. It was a treacherous act that angered King Charles V. Such an atrocity punctured Spain's claim that it had a moral and religious right to rule the Americas.

The execution of the emperor was the decisive turn for the Spanish conquest. Pizarro next marched south and took control of the capital of Cuzco. With the land now leaderless, Pizarro placed Atahualpa's other brother, Manco Capac, on the throne as a puppet ruler who would take orders from the Spaniards. But Manco never accepted the role of puppet ruler. He organized a rebellious movement that fought on for decades. It would not end until 1572, when the Andean leader Tupac Amaru was executed by the Spanish.

Meanwhile, violent quarrels broke out between Pizarro and his partner Almagro over political control and the division of the loot. It ended years later, with Almagro's execution on July 8, 1538. And then, in turn, Almagro's friends assassinated Pizarro in his palace in Lima. His rule was brief—hardly ten years before he was murdered on July 26, 1541.

The loss of Pizarro didn't stop his family from carrying on business as usual. How did the Pizarros build their huge organization to run the empire they had taken over and to wring from it every bit of wealth possible?

They formed alliances with others, broke them when it suited their interests, created laws and regulations to satisfy their needs, and violated them when they didn't. Their influence reached into almost every corner

The murder of Pizarro

of the continent, and into Spain, as well. They created an international business enterprise with no concern for decency and honor. Let's look at just two of the Pizarro enterprises. The most important was mining. Silver mines were being worked before the arrival of the Spaniards. As more and more rich veins were uncovered, the Pizarros led a silver rush. The first miners, Indians who were paid wages, were replaced by forced labor. Working conditions became so appalling that the mines were compared to "a mouth of hell, into which a great mass of people enter every year and are sacrificed by the greed of the Spaniards." Mule trains loaded with silver wound over the Andes and down to the Pacific coast for shipment to Spain, where bullion from America was used to pay for the spices of the East. "The commercial explorations of Asia," said the historian Eugene Rice, "was made possible by the discovery of precious metals in the West."

In 1545 one of the richest silver deposits in the world was discovered at Potosí in the Bolivian highlands. Silver replaced gold as the principal export of Spanish America to Europe. Within twenty-five years, Potosí had a population of 120,000—larger than any city in Spain.

Was Spain's colonial mining any worse than others? It seems all sixteenth-century miners, whether in the Americas or elsewhere, were exploited with the same harshness and cruelty.

New technology imported from Germany in the mid-1500s greatly increased the yield of silver ores. In some fifteen years, production of silver quadrupled at Potosí. For the next three centuries, Potosí would be Europe's main source of silver bullion.

Another profitable industry was created around the coca plant. It was a commodity produced under oppressive conditions. The leaves of the coca bush were chewed by Peruvian Indians to produce a tiny amount of cocaine. Used as a mild stimulant, it could reduce hunger and fatigue. Coca grew not in the highland region of the Andean Indians, but far below, at the edge of humid forests. The Spanish planters

An engraving dated about 1670 suggests
the horrors of the silver mines at Potosí.

and merchants who controlled the lives of the highland natives forced them to work on the plantations. The switch in climate from the high altitude, where the natives' lungs had long evolved to breathe thin air, proved fatal when they labored thousands of feet below. They died of many diseases, including cancer. From one-third to one-half of the workers failed to survive the first five months of plantation labor.

But the coca trade was too profitable for any businessman to give it up voluntarily. Yet one Spaniard felt some guilt. He wrote that down in the coca plantations "there is one disease worse than all the rest: the unrestrained greed of the Spaniards."

To supplement the labor of the Indians, the Spaniards used black slaves. One of Pizarro's majordomos boasted in a letter that he now had sixty-four slaves, both blacks and Nicaraguan Indians. As the Indian population in Peru kept dropping rapidly, more black slaves were brought in to meet the labor needs of the Spanish. At one point there were fewer Spaniards than black slaves in Lima, the capital. Among the most important customers of the international slave trade were the merchants of Europe, who were supplying Spain's empire with slave labor. Charles V profited personally, by selling licenses to furnish his colonies with slaves.

In time there was hardly any level of Spanish Peruvian society—artisans, priests, lawyers, merchants, sailors, captains, and free blacks—that did not include owners of slaves. Even a relatively poor man might own a black slave and an Indian slave. Most black slaves were personal servants, although many worked in the migrant gangs organized for mining. Black slaves were also much in demand as highly skilled artisans. The historian James Lockhart says "blacks were a factor of absolutely first importance in Peru in the conquest period."

The fact that the clergy themselves owned thousands of slaves in the Spanish and Portuguese colonies was taken as proof that slavery

THE PATH TO POWER

The basic means of Spanish exploitation of Indian labor and products was the *encomienda*—a royal grant as reward for military service. To receive an encomienda meant that an individual received the tribute of Indians within a certain region, and in return was obligated to protect them and see to their religious welfare.

The encomienda was not a grant of land. The grant came not from the crown directly, but from the governor or viceroy. Soon after the conquest of Peru, the person granted an encomienda system was extended to include the right to use Indians in mines or agricultural enterprises. Even though the encomienda didn't own the land, his monopoly on labor made the land of little value to anyone else. From the seventeenth century on, the encomiendas were turning into the haciendas, or great estates, of Spanish America.

The first *encomenderos* of Peru were members of the conquering expedition of 1532. Peru was dominated by the Pizarro brothers. For example, Gonzalo Pizarro owned many houses, palaces, and great estates. He received the tribute of more than 8,000 Indians. Great crops of maize and coca were raised for him, and he had his own silver mine. Whole towns and provinces were under his control.

and the slave trade were legitimate. And why not? asked some. Doesn't it promote the spread of Catholic Christianity? Those who profited by slavery had no trouble finding arguments to defend the practice. Quoting the classical Greek philosopher Aristotle, those who were proslavery claimed that blacks were natural slaves, born for bondage. Others, making a more practical case, held that the slave trade couldn't be stopped without endangering the survival of the colonies and therefore the spreading of Christianity. So from Puerto Rico to Peru, slavery became a basic system of labor. However, in Peru, as in most parts of Latin America, Indian workers greatly outnumbered black slaves.

N I N E
The Struggle for Freedom

By the end of the sixteenth century, Spain was in complete control of its new colonies in South America. The native people of the Inca Empire continued to labor for the Spanish conquerors. About four out of five of the men came under the yoke of forced labor, in the mines or on the plantations. The wealth they produced out of the land's natural resources poured into private hands or the Spanish treasury. It is no wonder that the mass of Peruvians sank into poverty and despair.

The decline in Peru's population as a consequence of the Spanish invasion was appalling. The most obvious cause was disease, to which the Indians had no immunity. One estimate holds that at the time Pizarro arrived, the population numbered about 7 million. By the late sixteenth century it had dropped to approximately 1.8 million.

The indigenous people perished not only in Peru, but throughout North and South America. It has been estimated that as much as three-fourths of the pre-Columbian population had disappeared by 1650.

But disease was not the main cause of what some say approached genocide in Peru. In the first forty years of Spanish rule, the decline resulted more from cultural shock and chaotic administration, for the people had suffered a numbing series of catastrophes.

As anthropologists studying native peoples have reported, when times are turbulent, the people may become so deeply demoralized that they lose the will to live. Their way of life may collapse. Some of the Spanish king's emissaries to Peru sent back reports of the terrible exploitation suffered by the indigenous population of Peru in the hands of encomenderos, priests, and colonial authorities.

> *The injuries and injustices that have been and are being done to the poor docile Indians cannot be counted. Everything from the very beginning is injury. Their liberty had been removed; their nobles have lost their nobility, authority and all form of jurisdiction; the Spaniards have taken their pastures and many fine lands, and impose intolerable tributes on them . . .*

Another wrote,

> *The tributes and taxes they pay are endured only with great difficulty and hardship. Nothing is left over for them to have any leisure, to endure times of necessity or illness—as we Spaniards have—or to raise their children. They live in poverty and lack the necessities of life, and never finish paying debts of the balance of their tributes. We can see they are dying out and being consumed very rapidly.*

Tupac Amaru II, leader of a rebellion against Spanish rule
from 1780 to 1783

The Struggle for Freedom

The Inca people, from the beginning of the Spanish invasion, never resigned themselves to their fate. In the eighteenth century more than one hundred revolts in various parts of Peru broke out. Some were led by descendants of the Inca kings. One of these, Tupac Amaru II, launched the greatest challenge to Spain's rule, in 1780. At about age forty, he presented himself as the Inca and raised a rebellion. His independence movement rallied supporters in several parts of Peru, although some Inca nobles continued their subservience to the Spaniards.

After about three years of struggle costing 200,000 lives, Spain defeated the rebels and captured their leader and his family. In the same square where Atahualpa had been executed two centuries before, the Inca was made to watch as his wife, uncle, and eldest son had their tongues torn out and were then garroted. After a month of torture, Tupac Amaru II was chopped to pieces on the scaffold. Though he died, his followers in several parts of the empire fought on for another year, killing thousands of Spaniards in revenge. But in the end, the rebellion was crushed. And with the same fanatical intensity Spain had shown against the Jews in the late fifteenth century during the Inquisition, it did its best to destroy the culture and the integrity of the Indians of Peru.

Three hundred years after Pizarro, Peru finally was free of Spanish domination and became independent. That happened when Simón Bolívar (1783–1830) led forces in several Latin American countries that won freedom from Spain. Peru's independence was gained in 1824. The new leaders of the republic had no room for Incas. They believed that the Indians were no longer a distinct people but truly a class of serfs.

In the twentieth century cycles of civilian and military government's occurred, with modern Peru plagued by economic problems and frequent internal warfare. However, it would be more than another 170 years before the first Indian in Peru's history would be

Simón Bolívar, who led wars of Peruvian independence from Spain and several other countries of Latin America. Here he is shown liberating slaves in Colombia.

elected president, when Alejandro Toledo won the election in 2001.

Today, Peru has a population of more than 27 million. Three out of four people live in the cities. The Amerindians (American Indians) number 45 percent; the mestizo (people of European and American Indian ancestry), 37 percent; and whites, 15 percent. Both Spanish and Quechua are Peru's official languages. The population of Lima, the capital city, is 7.4 million.

What happened to the Incas has happened to other people throughout history. It often does whenever an outside power conquers a territory or nation and then exploits its people and its resources. Spain and almost every country in Europe has done it—in the Americas and in Africa, Asia, and Australia. If you need evidence closer to home, examine the history of the United States during those times when it has dominated other peoples or countries.

Pizarro and His Times

1475   Francisco Pizarro is born (the precise date is unknown).

1492   Columbus makes his first voyage to the New World.

1497   Amerigo Vespucci sails to South America.

1498   Vasco da Gama discovers a sea route to India.

1500   Juan Ponce de León lands in Florida.

1513   Vasco Núñez de Balboa, with Pizarro, reaches the Pacific Ocean.

1519   Hernán Cortés conquers Mexico.

1519–1521   Ferdinand Magellan circumnavigates the globe.

1524–1525   Pizarro embarks on his first voyage along the Pacific coast.

1526   In Panama, Pizarro enters a partnership with Almagro and Luque.

1527   Pizarro arrives on the island of Gallo.

1529   The Spanish crown grants Pizarro the right to conquer Peru.

1532   Pizarro leads an expedition from Panama to the Inca Empire in Peru. He captures and executes Atahualpa, the Inca emperor, and begins the conquest of Peru.

1541   Pizarro is murdered on July 26.

FURTHER RESEARCH

Books

De Angelis, Gina. *Francisco Pizarro and the Conquest of the Inca*. Broomall, PA: Chelsea House Publishing, 2000.

Malpass, Michael A. *Daily Life in the Inca Empire*. Westport, CT: Greenwood Publishing Group, 1996.

Manning, Ruth. *Francisco Pizarro*. Crystal Lake, IL: Heinemann Library, 2000.

Nishi, Dennis. *The Inca Empire*. San Diego, CA: Lucent Books, 2000.

Web Sites

The Conquest of the Inca Empire: Francisco Pizarro

http://www.acs.ucalgary.ca/applied_history/tutor/eurvoya/inca.html

PBS Conquistadors: Pizarro

http://www.pbs.org/conquistadors/pizarro_flat.html

BIBLIOGRAPHY

Barzun, Jacques. *From Dawn to Decadence: 500 Years of Western Cultural Life, 1500 to the Present*. New York: Harper Collins, 2000.

Boorstin, Daniel J. *The Discoverers*. New York: Vintage, 1985.

Braudel, Fernand. *Capitalism and Material Life: 1400–1800*. New York: Harper & Row, 1973.

———. *The Wheels of Commerce*. New York: Harper & Row, 1982.

Davies, Norman. *Europe: A History*. New York: Oxford University Press, 1996.

Davis, David Brion. *The Problem of Slavery in Western Culture*. Ithaca, NY: Cornell University Press, 1966.

Diamond, Jared. *Guns, Germs and Steel: The Fates of Human Societies*. New York: Norton, 1997.

Elliott, John Huxtable. *Spain and Its World: 1500–1700: Selected Essays*. New Haven, CT: Yale University Press, 1989.

Fagan, Brian M., ed. *The Oxford Companion to Archaeology*. New York: Oxford University Press, 1996.

Gabai, Rafael Varon. *Francisco Pizarro and His Brothers: The Illusion of Power in Sixteenth-Century Peru*. Norman, OK: Oklahoma University Press, 1997.

Hale, J. R. *Renaissance Europe*. Berkeley, CA: University of California Press, 1971.

Hemming, John. *The Conquest of the Incas*. San Diego: Harcourt Brace Jovanovich, 1970.

Hobsbawm, Eric J. *Uncommon People*. London: Weidenfeld & Nicholson, 1998.

Howard, Cecil. *Pizarro and the Conquest of Peru*. New York: American Heritage, 1968.

Landes, David S. *The Wealth and Poverty of Nations: Why Some Are So Rich and Some So Poor*. New York: Norton, 1998.

Lockhart, James. *Spanish Peru: 1532–1560. A Social History.* Madison, WI: University of Wisconsin Press, 1994.

Parry, J. H. *The Age of Reconnaissance.* Berkeley, CA: University of California Press, 1981.

———. *The Discovery of the Sea.* Berkeley, CA: University of California Press, 1981.

Pirenne, Henri. *A History of Europe, vol. 2: From the Thirteenth Century to the Renaissance and Reformation.* Garden City, NY: Doubleday, 1956.

Rice, Eugene F., Jr. *The Foundations of Early Modern Europe, 1460–1559.* New York: Norton, 1970.

Roberts, J. M. *The Penguin History of Latin America.* New York: Penguin, 1992.

Thomas, Hugh. *Conquest.* New York: Touchstone, 1993.

Williamson, Edwin. *The Penguin History of Latin America.* New York: Penguin, 1992.

Wissler, Clark. *Adventures in the Wilderness.* New Haven: Yale University Press, 1925.

Wolf, Eric. R. *Europe and the People Without History.* Berkeley, CA: University of California Press, 1982.

Wood, Michael. *Conquistadors.* Berkeley, CA: University of California Press, 2000.

Wright, Ronald. *Stolen Continents: The "New World" Through Indian Eyes.* Boston: Houghton Mifflin, 1992.

INDEX

Page numbers in **boldface** are illustrations.

Index